Chinese New Year

A WORLD OF HOLIDAYS

Chinese New Year

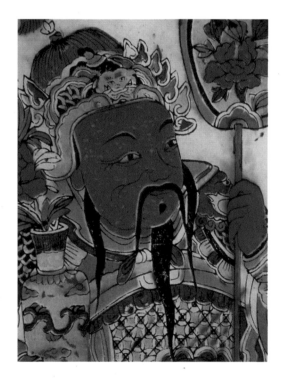

Catherine Chambers

RSVP
RAINTREE
STECK-VAUGHN
PUBLISHERS
The Steck-Vaughn Company

Austin, Texas

Published by Raintree Steck-Vaughn Publishers, an imprint of Steck-Vaughn Company

Library of Congress Cataloging-in-Publication Data

Chambers, Catherine.
  Chinese New Year / Catherine Chambers.
    p.   cm. — (A world of holidays)
  Includes bibliographical references (p.) and index.
  Summary: Describes the traditions, ceremonies, and foods associated with the celebration of the Chinese New Year.
    ISBN 0-8172-4605-3 (hardcover)
    ISBN 0-8172-3884-0 (softcover)
    1. Chinese New Year—Juvenile literature.   2. Chinese —Social life and customs—Juvenile literature.   I. Title. II. Series.
  GT4905.C42   1997
  394.261—dc20   96-34426
                                                 CIP
                                                   AC

Printed in Spain
Bound in United States
3 4 5 6 7 8 9 0   02 01

ACKNOWLEDGMENTS

Editor: Su Swallow, Pam Wells
Design: Neil Sayer
Production: Jenny Mulvanny

For permission to reproduce copyright material, the author and publishers gratefully acknowledge the following:

Title page Chapman Lee/Image Bank **page 6** Robert Harding Picture Library **page 7** (top) Robert Harding Picture Library (bottom) Chris Stowers/Panos Pictures **page 8** (background) Sally and Richard Greenhill (foreground) Trip/H Rogers **page 10** Robert Harding Picture Library **page 11** Chapman Lee/Image Bank **page 12** Trip/J Wakelin **page 13** (top) Mary Evans Picture Library (bottom) Robert Harding Picture Library **page 14** Emma Lee/Life File **page 15** Juliet Highet/Life File **page 17** (top) Maurice Harvey/Hutchison Library (bottom) Margaret Collier/Robert Harding Picture Library **page 18** Sarah Murray/Hutchison Library **page 19** Guido Rossi/Image Bank **page 20** G. Corrigan/ Robert Harding Picture Library **page 21** (top) Martha Cooper/Viesti Associate, Inc. (bottom) Robert Harding Picture Library **page 23** (top right) Trip/A Tovey (middle) Zefa **page 24** Sarah Murray/Hutchison Library **page 25** Jeremy Hoare/Life File **page 26** (top) Joseph Brignola/Image Bank (bottom) Mary Evans Picture Library **page 27** Trip/J Moscrop **page 28/29** Alan Towse Photography **page 30** Paul Van Riel/Robert Harding Picture Library

Contents

Harvests and Happiness   6

Animal Antics   8

Rites and Rituals   10

A Holiday Diary   12

Fire and Light   16

Peachwood and Poems   18

Drums and Dancing   20

Special Foods and Feasts   22

Faraway Celebrations   24

Lighting Lanterns   26

Let's Celebrate!   28

Glossary   30

Further Reading   30

Index   31

Harvests and Happiness

With gongs and dancing, flowers and firecrackers, the Chinese New Year warms the cold winter. The New Year is also known as the Spring Festival, bringing hopes for a good harvest in the year to come.

New Year calendars are on sale in the Chinese part of a large Western city. Red is a lucky color for the Chinese.

WHO CELEBRATES?

Throughout most of China, Taiwan, and Hong Kong, Chinese New Year explodes in city streets and in the countryside. Chinese people living in other parts of the world also celebrate the New Year with flowers and firecrackers and special foods.

Chinese New Year's Day is a public holiday for the whole country. Many people like to celebrate for several days.

TIME TO CELEBRATE

Chinese New Year starts somewhere between January 21 and February 19. The date changes from year to year because it follows an ancient calendar based on the phases of the moon. This is called a lunar calendar.

In southern China, bundles of grain are being turned so that they dry completely. During the Spring Festival the farmer will be hoping that the next year's crop is just as good as this one.

A lion dancer is going to do battle with another lion or maybe a rooster. Sometimes there are monkey dancers and clowns, too. Lion dances take place in Chinese communities throughout the world, from California to Calcutta.

❧ Animal Antics ❧

Every new year in China is named after one of twelve animals, each animal taking a year in turn. The year 2000 will be the Year of the Dragon! Animal signs are used for holidays and religious ceremonies, birthdays, and for working out horoscopes. Look at the birth-year animals. Which one are you?

If you start with the Rat and move to the right, you will follow the cycle of years. To find out which animals are which look on page 9.

AN ANIMAL ARGUMENT!

How did the animals decide who should start the cycle of years? Here is just one of the stories.

The animals were having an argument. Each of them wanted to be the very first Animal of the Year. So the gods said that the animals must have a race across a river. The winner would start the cycle of years.

All the animals leaped into the water together. But the strong Ox soon took the lead. The other animals struggled behind him—all except Rat. No one had noticed him crouched on Ox's back. Just before Ox touched the other side, Rat leaped onto the bank and won the race!

Rat 1972, 1984, 1996 You have a hot temper but a lot of charm. You always finish what you set out to do.

Ox 1973, 1985, 1997 You are quiet, calm, and can keep a secret. You like doing things on your own.

Tiger 1974, 1986, 1998 You are brave and have a strong will. You are loving but can get somewhat angry at times.

Rabbit 1975, 1987, 1999 You are lucky but deserve it because you are patient and not greedy. You are shy and a bit moody sometimes.

Dragon 1976, 1988, 2000 You like to be the leader—you talk a lot and sometimes ask a bit too much of other people. You can be sensitive.

Snake 1977, 1989, 2001 You are wise and attractive, but sometimes you boast. You can also be a little mean.

Horse 1978, 1990, 2002 You are independent, clever, and people admire you. You are cheerful and like talking!

Ram 1979, 1991, 2003 You are artistic, calm, and caring. You also know how to use your talents well. But you can't always make up your mind!

Monkey 1980, 1992, 2004 You have a lot of good in you. You are creative and successful, but you can cause trouble!

Rooster 1981, 1993, 2005 You are clever and hardworking. Sometimes you like to be alone, dreaming of great things. You are usually modest—but not always.

Dog 1982, 1994, 2006 You are very hardworking and loyal. Justice is important to you. But you have quite a strong will.

Pig 1983, 1995, 2007 You have a strong character—in a quiet sort of way. You like to learn—but only about the things that interest you.

～ Rites and Rituals ～

For many people, Chinese New Year is a religious festival as well as a lot of fun. It began long ago when there was only one religion that had many gods and spirits. Today, the New Year is also celebrated in the temples of newer faiths.

At this Buddhist temple, people will light joss sticks and say prayers for a peaceful New Year.

▶ This Door God guard was once a famous soldier. Every New Year people put up his picture to guard their homes.

GODS THAT GUARD YOU

The ancient Chinese religion had many Door Gods in the house to watch over the family. One story about a Door God guard takes us back a thousand years.

Emperor Taizong had fallen ill, and one night he lay tossing and turning in his bed. He had a really bad dream. Ghosts howled and screamed in his head all night. The next day he told his two best soldiers, Qin Qiong and Yuchi Gong, about the dream.

The next night, these good soldiers stood outside the emperor's bedroom door. One held a club and the other, an iron rod. In the morning, the emperor said that he had slept like a log. But the soldiers could not

spend every night guarding his room. So the emperor told an artist to paint pictures of the two soldiers. These were hung as guards on the palace gates.

Word soon got around that the paintings were guarding the palace against evil spirits. People started to place pictures of the two soldiers outside their homes, too. Today, at New Year, millions of Door God pictures flutter in the winter wind.

A Holiday Diary

Find out what happens at Chinese New Year by following this holiday diary! Long ago, the fun lasted for fifteen days. But now, most people celebrate only the first three days of the holiday.

BE PREPARED!
There's plenty of work to be done before the New Year fun begins. First, everyone helps to clean the house from top to bottom. Lots of food is prepared for New Year's Day. Lucky red decorations are hung over doors and around rooms. Flower fairs and gift stands are set up. All debts have to be paid back, too. This is not as important as it used to be. Long ago, people had to hide if they owed money to someone!

Flowers are a symbol of plenty at New Year. There are lots to choose from here!

The doors are sealed—nothing bad can get in now. The good luck stays inside.

NEW YEAR'S EVE

Not many people go to bed on New Year's Eve. The streets buzz with happy people, young and old alike. Temples are full of worshipers. Families gather from far and wide to eat a special meal together.

Some families still follow the old New Year traditions. They stay in the house and shut the doors and windows tight to keep evil spirits from getting in. Tree branches are burned, and firecrackers are set off to drive away the spirits. On New Year's morning the doors and windows are unlocked and good wishes are spoken. Now the New Year celebrations can really begin!

A wedding procession in northern China. This wedding took place during the New Year celebrations.

13

ON NEW YEAR'S DAY, YOU CAN ...

shout "Happy New Year!" and hope for wealth for everyone. Children hope to get little red envelopes with "lucky money" inside them! Families gather together—everyone wearing his or her new clothes. At the crowded dinner table, you won't see much meat. Many people do not eat meat on New Year's Day.

BUT ON NEW YEAR'S DAY YOU CANNOT...

wash! At least, people didn't in the past. They did take a long bath on New Year's Eve, though. You must not clean the house, either. If you do, all the wealth that the gods have brought for the new year will be swept away. Try not to break anything, because this will bring bad luck. Falling over or using bad language is also unlucky. And don't use any knives or scissors either!

ON THE SECOND DAY...

people visit family and friends. Some go gambling. New Year is the only time when gambling is not frowned upon.

ON THE THIRD DAY...

don't go visiting people. It's bound to end up in an argument! But you could visit a temple and find out your future with fortune sticks.

These Chinese dolls are a very special decoration. They're holding New Year money envelopes with clasped hands. The hands show that they greet people with good wishes for the future.

Red and gold are lucky colors used on these money envelopes.

ON THE FOURTH DAY...

most people start returning to normal. But teams of dancers dress up and dance in the streets. (See page 20.)

FROM THE FIFTH TO THE FIFTEENTH DAY...

you can clean the house and get back to work now. You can go to the sales to look for bargains. All the gods in heaven gather together on the eighth day. Some people ask for their blessings. On the ninth day, you might burn some incense for the birthday of the Jade Emperor, the king of the gods. Finally, between the tenth and the fifteenth days, you can buy lanterns with good wishes written on them. The Lantern Festival ends the New Year celebrations. Find out more about it on page 26!

People in Hong Kong are choosing fortune sticks to take to the temple. The way the sticks fall shows the kind of luck the person will have.

Fire and Light

Millions of firecrackers explode and sparkle on New Year's Day. Today they are really just for fun. Long ago, they were set off to keep away evil spirits in the year to come.

GHOSTS, MONSTERS, AND EVIL SPIRITS

Now, firecrackers bring joy and laughter. But in ancient times, people believed that the noise and bright lights of the firecrackers chased away ghosts and devils, too. They also frightened off a huge mountain giant. At the end of the old year, this angry beast came down from the mountain to kill every living creature in sight. But people noticed that it was scared of flashes of light and loud bangs. So bamboo stems were set on fire to make the monster run right back up the mountain.

THE FIRST FIRECRACKERS

In ancient times, people set fire to bamboo stems. The stems are hollow inside except for joints along their length. When the bamboo is lit, the air inside the stems expands. The pressure is so great, the bamboo suddenly splits open with a loud crack. Today, fireworks are created and handled carefully by experts.

QUIET LIGHT

Many people visit temples during the Spring Festival to pray for peace and success. They also light hundreds of joss sticks for good luck. The word *joss* was brought to China by early Portuguese explorers. It was actually *Deos,* which means "God." Joss sticks are made of thin strips of bamboo cane dipped in sawdust and sweet-smelling powder made from tree gums.

Fireworks displays light up the harbor in Hong Kong during New Year celebrations.

People light joss sticks in a Chinese temple in Malaysia.

Peachwood and Poems

In ancient times, charms made of peachwood were lucky symbols. Rhymes of good fortune were written on them. Now, these rhymes are printed on strips of red paper. They are stuck on doors all over the house.

IMPORTANT PEACHES

More than a thousand years ago, New Year messages were written on small peachwood charms. They were hung on gates to protect the home. Later, these short messages were written as two-line poems, called Spring couplets.

The Chinese writing for "peach" also means long life, so peaches are thought to be lucky. At New Year, people buy a small peach tree, or some peach blossoms.

RHYMES ON RED PAPER

Today, these poems are printed on red paper. They are placed around the home, especially on doors. Here are some of the verses of hope for the future:

Peaceful days throughout the years
Spring of good luck forever

May your happiness be as wide as the East Sea

May you have a favorable wind all the way

▶ No wonder this woman is smiling! Her doorway is surrounded by hopeful messages on red paper. People wish for peace, wealth, a long life, many children, and even power.

Drums and Dancing

Gongs, drums, and cymbals ring and crash throughout New Year, especially in southern China. Dancers in animal and clown costumes mime, somersault, or walk on stilts.

DEAFENING DRUMS!

In the south of China, villages take part in the New Year drum competitions. Each band has a drum, a pair of cymbals, and several gongs. A team plays to the rhythms of its own drum, but all the bands perform at the same time. The music thunders like cannons as each band tries to overpower all the others!

DANCING LIONS

Between the fourth and the fifteenth days of the New Year, teams of dancers tour the countryside. Each team has about ten dancers, all dressed in the same trousers, jackets, and hats. They are armed with swords and clubs, just like soldiers. But among these dancers come bright paper heads of lions, cats, and roosters, decorated with ringing bells.

Dancers hold the animals' heads and move them to the sound of

Up in the mountains in Qinghai province, expert stilt dancers parade down the street in bright costumes.

drums and gongs. Their bodies leap in the air or roll on the ground, moving like the beasts they are meant to be. Dancers in monkey and clown costumes twist, somersault, and joke in front of the crowd.

20

A New Year dragon
dance in New York.

A New Year lion dance.

❧ Special Foods and Feasts ❧

Mounds of sticky cakes and plump dumplings are eaten during the Spring Festival! The vast farming areas of China produce an enormous variety of foods. These are made into favorite dishes at this time of year.

PREPARING FOR A PARTY

It takes a long time to prepare food for the long New Year festivities. In the south, piles of rice grains are sorted and washed several days before the celebrations. This way, the job will be done on time. The huge mounds of rice are a symbol of hope for a good harvest next year.

Dates, chestnuts, walnuts, hazelnuts, melon seeds, lotus seeds, and oranges are favorite snacks. The word used for each often sounds like a word meaning something lucky.

Duck, chicken, and goose are favorite holiday meats. But people do not just eat it all greedily. Meat and fish are also taken to shrines and offered to the gods and spirits.

SWEET SUCCESS

On New Year's Eve and New Year's Day in northern China, sweet dumplings are shaped like the golden shoes that were used as money in ancient China. If you are really lucky, you might find a coin in your dumpling!

In southern China, people believe that eating lots of sticky cakes brings good luck.

Fruit is very popular at New Year, especially mandarin oranges.

Many people enjoy Won Ton soup at New Year.

Faraway Celebrations

Chinese New Year is not only celebrated in China! In other parts of Southeast Asia and in cities from New York to Vancouver, Chinese communities put on their biggest festival.

A SCATTERED PEOPLE

Chinese people have been leaving China's mainland for hundreds of years. Most went to other parts of Southeast Asia, such as Vietnam, Hong Kong, and Malaysia.

About 150 years ago, some Chinese left for America, Canada, and Australia. Here, they worked on the railroads or in gold mines.

Chinese communties can also be found in other countries, such as Great Britain. The city areas where they live are called Chinatown. Here, many Chinese people still follow their traditional ways.

People are buying decorations for New Year in a Chinatown in Europe.

Dazzling lights in Singapore show that New Year has arrived!

CHINESE NEW YEAR FAR AWAY

In New York's Chinatown, New Year brings dragon dancers and exploding firecrackers to the streets. There are about 400 Chinese restaurants in this small area. At this time of year they offer great feasts.

Do you like being scared? If so, you can follow the 82-foot-(25-m) long fierce dragon in San Francisco's Golden Dragon Parade. In Malaysia, on the fifteenth day of the festival, women throw oranges into the ocean. It is supposed to help them find a good husband. Chinese opera, with singing, cymbals, and gongs is performed free on the streets.

In Hong Kong, the children chant a special New Year rhyme wishing for lots of money wrapped up in lucky red envelopes. But the rhyme also wishes for happiness for everyone. This is the true spirit of Chinese New Year wherever it is celebrated.

Lighting Lanterns

The Lantern Festival is a bright and happy way to end the long celebrations. It takes place under the light of the New Year's first full moon.

THE LANTERN FESTIVAL LONG AGO

More than 2,000 years ago, people swung lanterns under the full moon on the fifteenth day of the New Year. Spring was getting closer, days were longer, and the

▶ This lantern in lucky red and gold has a prayer of hope written on it.

This is how a lantern shop looked more than 150 years ago.

sun a little stronger. So the celebration took place in honor of the Sun God, then known as the Lord of the East.

About 500 years later, the festival also marked the day when a cruel ruler was driven from power. The wise and kind Emperor Wen had taken over. Every year, on the night of the Lantern Festival, he went out onto the streets to celebrate the freedom of his people.

DECORATIONS AND DANCING

Today city streets, homes, stores, restaurants, and marketplaces glow with colored lights. In villages, lanterns are tied to strings and then hung in a tent shape from a strong pole. Animal lanterns, especially dragons, are carried along the streets in long processions. Families gather to watch masked dancers parading around the towns and villages.

Lantern frames are made of bamboo, wood, iron, wheat stalks, or even animal horn. They are covered with thin colored paper, silk, glass, or plastic. In the cold northeast, lights shine through shapes carved from ice. But perhaps the most beautiful are the colorful paper figures that spin around the bright light of a candle.

A paper-lantern market is full of lucky red and gold lanterns.

27

⋘ Let's Celebrate! ⋙

Join in the fun! Try making this lion mask and lucky red envelope. You can get lots of ideas by looking at the pictures of lion masks and lucky envelopes in the book.

MAKING A LION MASK

Materials:

- a large open cardboard box
- some poster paints and a brush
- sticky tape and glue or paste
- safe scissors
- materials to decorate your lion

You could paint strips of newspaper, or you could use aluminum foil, wool, ribbon, tissue paper, crêpe paper, or sequins.... Anything goes!

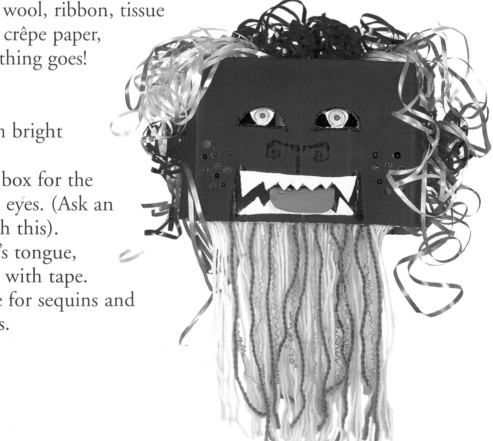

Directions:

1. Paint your box in bright colors.
2. Cut holes in the box for the lion's mouth and eyes. (Ask an adult to help with this).
3. Stick on the lion's tongue, mane, and beard with tape.
4. Use paste or glue for sequins and other decorations.

MAKING A LUCKY
RED ENVELOPE

Materials:
- a sheet of paper
- red and yellow paint and a brush
- safe scissors
- paste or glue

Directions:
1. Cut out your paper in the shape shown in the diagram.
2. Paint your paper red on one side.
3. Fold the side flaps in along the dotted lines in the diagram.
4. Fold up the bottom half of the paper along the dotted line.
5. Glue the flaps to the inside of the bottom half.
6. Stick a yellow lucky shape on your envelope. Fat, leaping fish, plump grain, and bouncing babies are all lucky!

Your lucky red envelope will look like this.

29

Glossary

Blessings Wishes of joy and happiness.

Celebrate To show that a certain day or event is special.

Celebration Ways of showing that a day or event is special, such as parades or parties.

Ceremonies Ways of celebrating a special event or day. Sometimes they are more solemn and serious than a celebration.

Communities Groups of people who live and work together.

Horoscope A description of a person's future and character. This description often uses their birth date and the position of the stars.

Procession A long line of people walking or dancing along a street.

Spirits Beings that you cannot see, something like ghosts.

Traditional Describes very old ways of living that parents teach to their children.

Worshipers People who show respect to gods and spirits through prayers and songs.

Further Reading

Chin, Steven A. *Dragon Parade: A Chinese New Year Story* (Stories of America series). Raintree Steck-Vaughn, 1992.

Flint, David. *China* (On the Map series). Raintree Steck-Vaughn, 1993.

Ganeri, Anita, *I Remember China* (Why We Left series) Raintree Steck-Vaughn, 1994.

Kalman, Bobbie. *We Celebrate New Year.* Crabtree, 1985.

MacMillan, Dianne M. *Chinese New Year* (Best Holiday Books series). Enslow, 1994.

Sing, Rachel. *Chinese New Year's Dragon.* Simon and Schuster Childrens, 1994.

Index

America 24
animal 7, 8, 9, 20, 21, 27
Australia 24

calendars 6
Canada 24
China 6, 7, 13, 22

dancers, dancing 7, 15, 20, 27
Door Gods 10
dragons 8, 9, 25, 27

firecrackers 6, 13, 16, 25
fireworks 16, 17
flowers 6, 12, 18

food 6, 12, 13, 14, 22, 23
fortune sticks 14, 15

gods 10, 15, 22, 27
Great Britain 24

harvest 6
Hong Kong 6, 15, 17, 24, 25

joss sticks 10, 16, 17

lantern 21, 26, 27
lucky red envelopes 14, 25

Malaysia 17, 24

mandarin oranges 23
music 20

New York 25

peach blossom 18

rhymes 18

spirits 10, 13, 16, 22

Taiwan 6
temples 10, 13, 17

Vietnam 24